Algae

BY HAROLD E. SCHLICHTING, JR.
MARY SOUTHWORTH SCHLICHTING

Illustrated by EARL YOUNG

STECK-VAUGHN COMPANY
An Intext Publisher
Austin, Texas

ISBN 0-8114-7720-7
Library of Congress Catalog Card Number 74-139289
Copyright © 1971 by Steck-Vaughn Company, Austin, Texas
All Rights Reserved
Printed and Bound in the United States of America

TABLE OF CONTENTS

INTRODUCTION

There are thousands of different kinds of algae living in the world.

You may have seen different kinds of algae (*al*-gee) and called them "pond scum." But algae are living things that have an interesting story.

Algae live almost everywhere. They are in oceans, lakes, rivers, swamps, and springs. They can be found in the soil, on rocks, trees, and buildings, as well as in the air. Algae also live in ice, snow, and in springs of water almost hot enough to boil. They can grow on or in animals such as fish, snails, clams, frogs, turtles, birds, and mammals.

Algae can be colorless or have one or several colors. They can grow in many different shapes and sizes. They can be invisible or as long as some redwood trees are high.

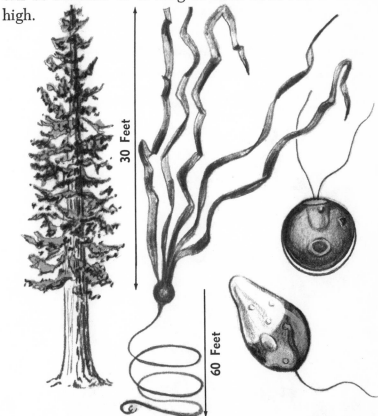

Many of the algae that live in water can move about. Movements of some of the small algae can be seen with the microscope. Some algae swim through the water like snakes. Others have a *flagellum* (fluh-*jel*-um), much like a tail of a tadpole, which pushes or pulls them through the water. It is thought that some algae may move like jet airplanes, shooting liquids or gases out small openings to project themselves.

5

CLASSIFICATION

Plants are grouped together, or classified, because of certain likenesses.

Algae are classified as plants because they can make their own food from water, soil, and air in the same way that trees, flowers, and other plants do.

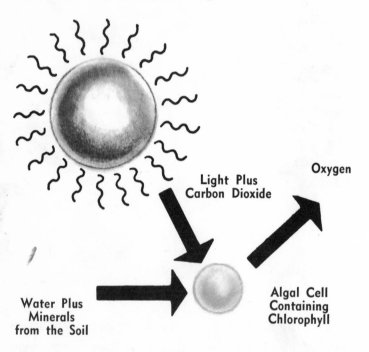

Light Plus
Carbon Dioxide

Oxygen

Water Plus
Minerals
from the Soil

Algal Cell
Containing
Chlorophyll

All algae have a special green pigment, a substance called "chlorophyll" (*klo*-ruh-fil) which permits them to manufacture their food. As in other plants, this process—which uses the energy of sunlight—is known as "photosynthesis" (fo-to-*syn*-thu-sis). Plant food is made up of sugar and starch.

Color is a means by which different types of algae are grouped. The five major divisions of algae are blue-green, green, red, brown, and golden-brown. There are other algae with other colors or no color. Even though they do not always appear green, all algae possess the green pigment, chlorophyll.

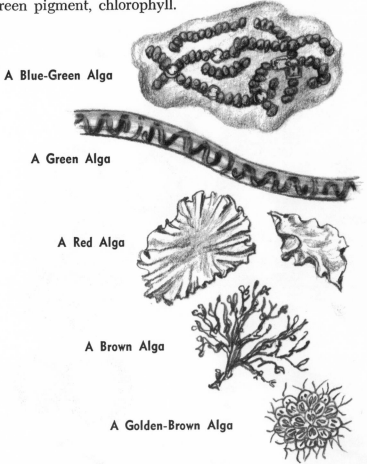

A Blue-Green Alga

A Green Alga

A Red Alga

A Brown Alga

A Golden-Brown Alga

Some of the algae are not always considered plants. They are sometimes grouped with other organisms such as bacteria or microscopic animals.

Shapes of algae are also used in classification. Even though many algae are made up of only one cell, they can have different shapes, such as stars, needles, pyramids, cubes, round balls, eggs, long threads, vases, and worms.

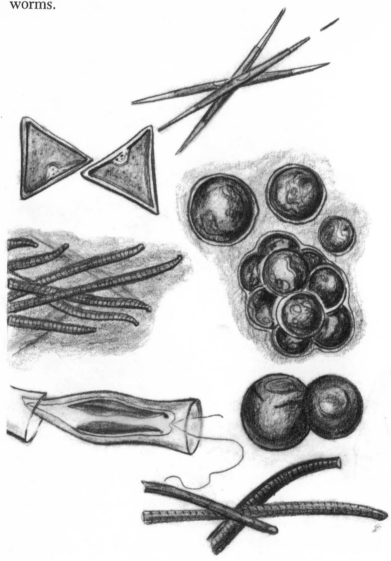

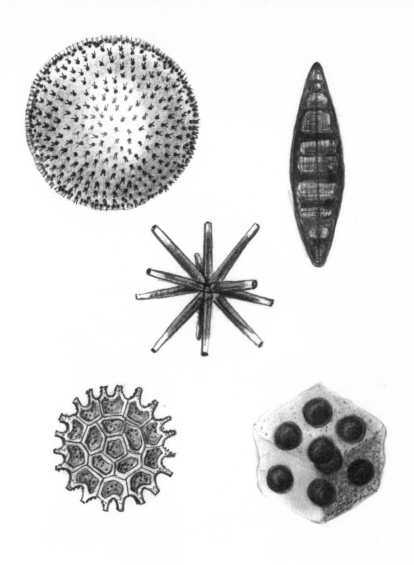

Others may group together in a colony. These colonies
may be shaped as a hollow ball, a diamond, a star, a
cube, or a flat plate.

9

Larger algae, made up of many cells, may be shaped like small bushes, palm trees, whips, leaves, tubes, and flat ribbons.

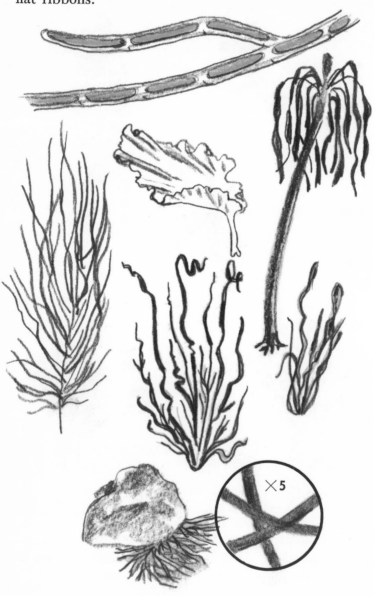

Sizes of algae vary. Those that float in the water are some of the smallest plants. Many can only be seen with a magnifying lens or microscope.

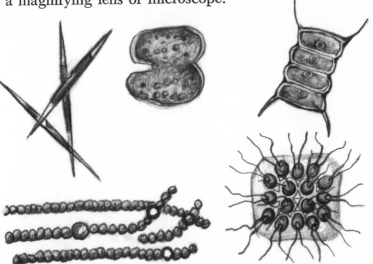

Some of the algae are very large, especially the seaweeds living in the oceans. They may reach 100 feet or more in length.

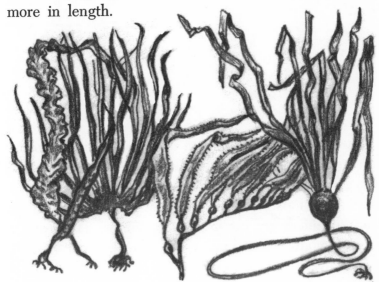

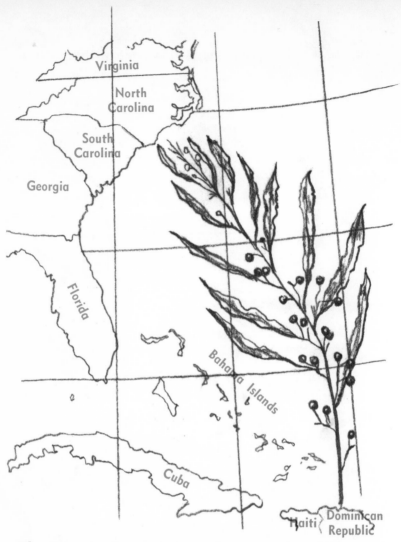

The Sargasso Sea is an area of very clear water in the Atlantic Ocean east of the Bahama Islands. Species of *Sargassum* grow abundantly in this area, forming large floating clumps many miles across. Numerous small marine animals and fish live in the clumps. These plants are commonly washed up on the beaches from Virginia to Mexico.

12

LIFE CYCLES OF ALGAE

*All of life's complex activities are
carried on inside both small and large algae.*

Algae can change in shape, size, and color during
their lifetime or life cycle. The change in color is often
because of age, but sometimes it is brought about by
the effect of light, temperature, or some other condition
in the area in which the algae may live.

There are three ways algae may form other plants like
themselves *asexually* (methods without the union of male
and female cells):

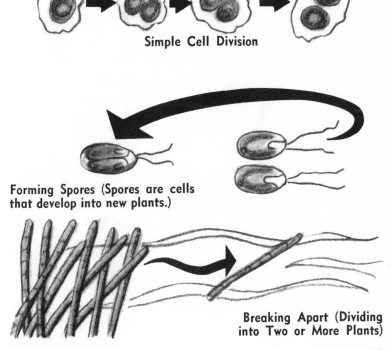

Simple Cell Division

**Forming Spores (Spores are cells
that develop into new plants.)**

**Breaking Apart (Dividing
into Two or More Plants)**

13

Algae also produce other plants like themselves by *sexual* methods. The parent plant releases special cells called "gametes" (*gam*-etes). They join together and grow into new parent cells.

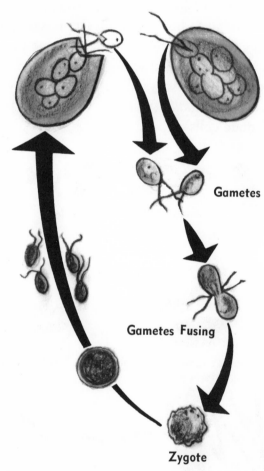

Gametes

Gametes Fusing

Zygote

A zygote (*zy*-goat) is a cell formed by two gametes joining together.

Some algae grow new plants by another type of sexual reproduction.

Such a plant is a brown alga, a large leaf-shaped plant which forms swimming cells called "zoospores" (*zo*-uh-spores) that move about in the water. These grow into two types of short threads or filaments which produce the gametes. One thread produces female cells, *eggs;* and the other produces the male cells, *sperm.* These join together, attach to the bottom of the ocean, and become a small leaf-shaped plant. In time it grows into a large plant.

Zoospore

Zoospore

Plant Producing
Sperm

Mature
Spore-Producing
Plant

Plant Producing
Eggs

Fused Sperm
and Egg

Zygote

Young
Spore-Producing
Plant

WHERE DO ALGAE LIVE?

Most algae live in water.

The most obvious place to look for algae is in water: puddles, ponds, lakes, rivers, and oceans. Just as land plants grow in certain areas, algae grow in special locations in the water. Some algae float about. Others attach themselves to sticks, rocks, larger plants, or the bottom of the body of water. Some algae grow best where the salt content of the water is high. Others need currents or waves, while some grow best in very still or slowly moving water. Different algae are to be found at different depths in the water at different times of the day and year.

Whenever you are near a body of water, notice how many different kinds of algae you can see.

16

Some algae grow in soil.

Different kinds of algae grow in different types of soil, such as garden soil, beach sand, mud, peat, and forest soil. Most algae grow best in the top inch of soil. Green algae are usually the most plentiful in soil. Golden-brown and blue-green algae can also be found in soil.

A few kinds of soil algae can also grow in total darkness and may be found at considerable depths beneath the surface. The nutrients for growth are in the soil, and the algae do not need to manufacture food.

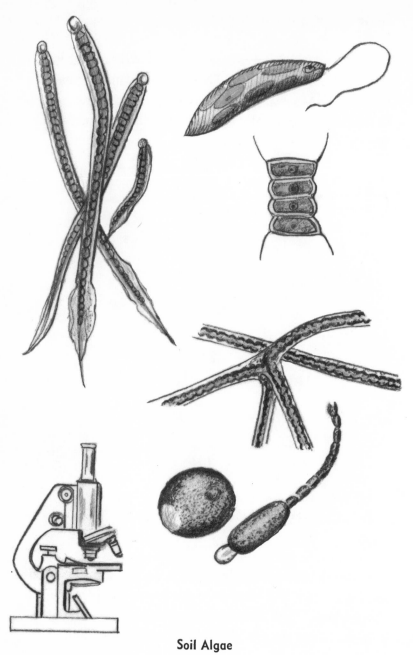

Soil Algae

Some algae grow on surfaces exposed to air.

Algae have also been found in the air we breathe. Winds carry the algae as well as the dust from one area to another. Aerial algae are commonly found on trees, fence posts, rocks, and buildings—especially if the climate is moist.

In Ireland, castles and churches built hundreds of years ago have several different kinds of algae growing on them. Green, yellow-orange, or red powder—which usually are older green algae—may appear on the walls. Patches of blue-green and golden-brown algae may also appear.

Are there algae growing on the walls or windowsills of your house or school?

Algae may grow on other forms of life.

Algae may also live on or inside other plants or animals. Some small flatworms living in ponds may be green in color due to the algae living in their bodies.

Sponges and other animals in the ocean sometimes have a green color because algae are living in their bodies.

Several kinds of algae have been found growing on the shells of turtles both in fresh water and in the oceans.

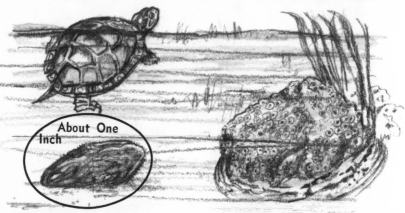

About One Inch

The South American tree sloth is green because algae are growing on its fur.

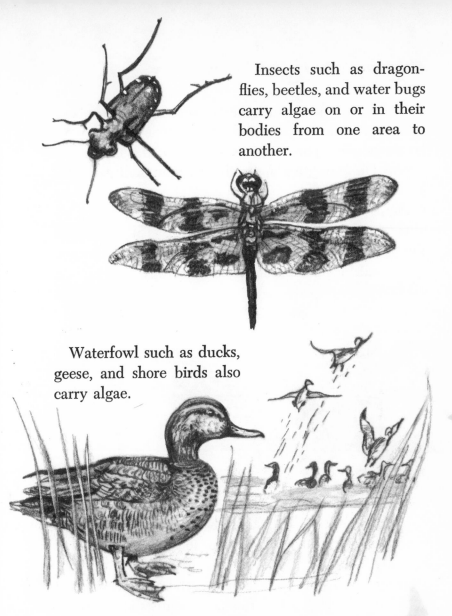

Insects such as dragon-flies, beetles, and water bugs carry algae on or in their bodies from one area to another.

Waterfowl such as ducks, geese, and shore birds also carry algae.

Algae grow on fish. Algae are also the main source of food for fish. Some of the plants are digested by the fish while others pass out of the fish's body alive and are able to grow in the water.

21

Algae may grow in plant combinations.

Lichens (*lie*-kens) are plants made up of two plants living together. One part of the lichen is an alga, a green, food-producing part. The other part of the lichen is a *fungus* (*fung*-us), a plant without chlorophyll that lives with the alga.

These unusual partners are often seen growing on trees, rocks, buildings, and the ground. They may look like small trees, bushes, or crusts. You may have seen them used for plants in model train setups.

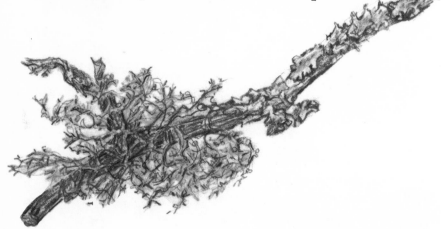

Acids produced by lichens help break the rock of mountains into soil. They may be able to dissolve cement.

Other lichens are used to make dyes and cosmetics. Reindeer eat lichens, and Russian scientists are working to develop cattle feeds from the plants since they are very plentiful in northern Russia. Lichens are also abundant in northern Canada and the Scandinavian countries, and they are found in most parts of the world.

Algae grow in unexpected places.

Algae grow in unusual places. Some blue-green algae can grow in the very hot water of pools in Yellowstone National Park.

Algae can also grow in ice and snow. Patches of green, orange, red, or yellow-brown may appear on the snow in the mountains. These colored patches are often caused by green algae.

HOW TO COLLECT AND PREPARE ALGAE FOR STUDY

It is fun to collect various types of algae.

Pick out some of the scum or threads of algae from a shallow pond or stream. Place the threads in clean jars which have been half filled with pond water that has been boiled and allowed to cool, or collect the threads in small plastic bags and close them with rubber bands.

Loosen the bands or lids of the jars when you arrive home. This will help keep the algae alive. Be sure that the jars you use have been washed and rinsed carefully before placing the algae in them.

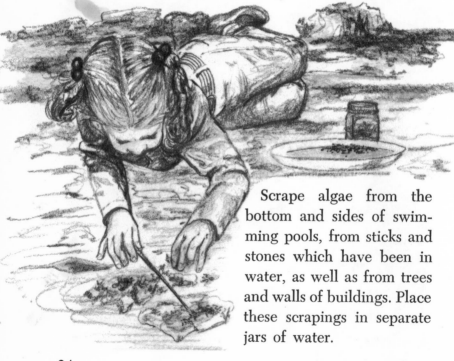

Scrape algae from the bottom and sides of swimming pools, from sticks and stones which have been in water, as well as from trees and walls of buildings. Place these scrapings in separate jars of water.

24

The free-floating forms of algae can be studied by collecting a jar of water from a pond or stream and allowing the organisms to settle to the bottom of the jar. Carefully pour off the top part of the water to concentrate the material for study. Some of the algae may collect on the water surface along the edge of the jar. Scrape off the material for study.

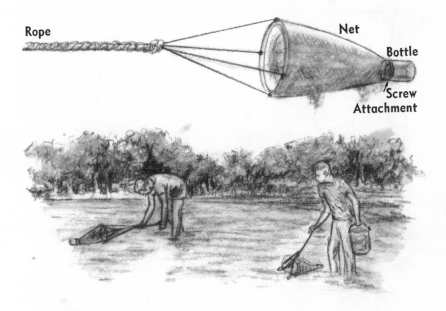

A plankton net is the best way to collect the small floating algae from water. The net, made of fine silk, catches the small algae as the net is pulled through the water. When the net is lifted out of the water, most of the water drains out of the net. The algae are trapped in a small bottle at the base in a small amount of water. The algae from the bottle may then be examined with a hand lens or microscope.

To study soil algae, place small amounts of different types of soil in clean glass jars. Label the jars.

| Top Soil from the Garden | Sand from the Beach or Sandpile | Dirt from under the Leaves in the Woods |

Add enough cool, boiled pond water to cover the soil in the jars. Place a piece of clear plastic loosely over the top and set the jars on a windowsill. Usually within two weeks a green, yellow-green, blue-green, or brown film will appear over the surface of the soil and along the edges of the jars. What colors can you find?

Carefully pick up land insects such as butterflies, grasshoppers, and ladybugs with clean forceps and rinse in a jar of cool, boiled water. Do the same with water insects: water boatmen, water striders, and others.

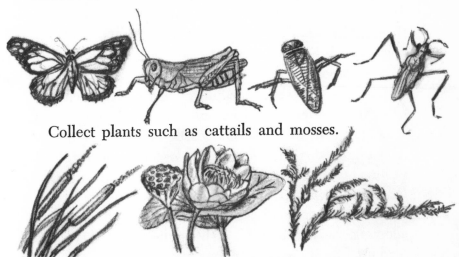

Collect plants such as cattails and mosses.

Collect animals: snails, fish, tadpoles, and frogs from the lake or from the fishbowl.

Wash the plants and animals in separate jars of cool, boiled pond water. Label the jars.

Place snow and ice in clean, loosely covered jars. Keep them at room temperature in a well lighted place.

Expose jars of cool, boiled pond water for different time lengths to the air. Keep the jars in a cool place where they will have light, but not direct sunlight.

You can help the algae grow.

Many times it is necessary to give the algae food to help them grow so that they are easier to see and study. The algae need special food to be healthy. Their food is called "media." *Soil-water medium* is the least expensive and the easiest to make. It is also best suited for most kinds of algae.

To make soil-water medium, collect some rich soil from the garden, removing all the small stones and crumbling the dirt into fine particles. Place about ¼ inch of the dirt into screw-top jars about half full of water. Loosen the lids slightly and steam the jars *over low heat* in a pan partly filled with water. Steam for one hour on two consecutive days. On the second day, after allowing the jars to cool, tighten the lids to keep the medium free from any contamination.

Add the algae, soil, or wash water from your various collections to jars containing the medium. You are now ready to watch the algae grow.

HOW TO STUDY ALGAE

Some algae may be studied when they are first collected. The scum and threads floating on the surface of the water may be seen better if placed in a shallow white pan containing a small amount of clear water.

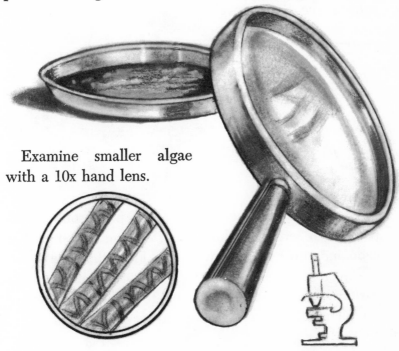

Examine smaller algae with a 10x hand lens.

Look at your fresh water algae from a pond with a microscope. Can you find long chains of cells? What appears green within the spiral band of the cells? Drop a few drops of iodine solution on your fresh water algae. They will turn blue-black, showing that they store starch as food. Does this give you a clue as to what the green bands contain? (Do you remember how all algae make their own food?)

If you have collected a common marine brown alga, you can test it to see if this type of brown algae truly contains the green pigment, chlorophyll.

Drop a small piece of the alga in boiling water. Watch for changes in the color of both water and plant. Brown pigment may be dissolved in water. What does the final color of the plant prove?

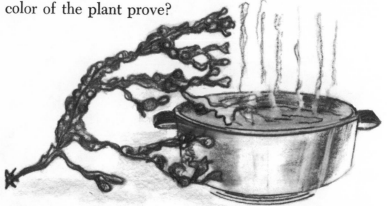

To examine the free-floating algae, place some of the plants that settled to the bottom of your jar on a glass slide and cover with a cover slip. Place the slide under the microscope and study the cells of the plant. Note various colors and sizes. Look for different views of the plant cells: top, side, and end views.

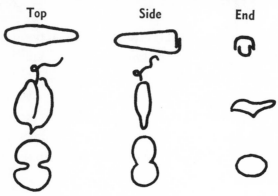

Top   Side   End

Wrap aluminum foil around a covered jar of water containing algae. Make a small hole in the foil near the top of the jar and place the jar about one foot from a lamp, with the hole facing the light. Leave for two days. Remove the algae attracted to the light with a clean medicine dropper and examine with a hand lens or microscope. What algae were attracted to the light?

After algae have grown for two to four weeks in media or water, pour the algal material on a pan of sand in which radish or tomato seeds have been planted. Add the same amount of plain media or water to another pan containing the same type and number of seeds. What effect do the algae have on the growth of the plants?

Algae in Water   Plain Water

Remove the growth of algae from the collecting jars and dry in an oven, using low heat. Feed small pieces of the dried algae to goldfish or minnows that you have collected. Do the fish eat the dried algae?

Did the fish eating the algae live? Did they grow as fast as those fish that ate fish food purchased from the store?

WHAT USES DO THE ALGAE HAVE?

Algae provide oxygen.

When carrying on photosynthesis during the daytime, algae produce more oxygen than they use. The large amounts of oxygen given off by the algae are used by all living things.

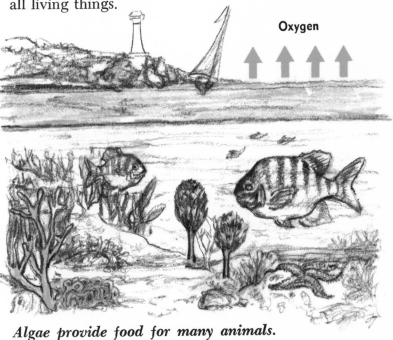

Oxygen

Algae provide food for many animals.

Algae are a greater source of food than the crops harvested each year by all the farmers throughout the entire world. Floating on the surface of the water, algae are a main source of food for all water-living animals, as well as some land animals. For this reason, algae are often called "the great meadow of the sea."

The transfer of food from one organism to another is called a "food chain."

Microscopic animals living in the water eat the algae. Whales and some fish also eat algae. Larger fish eat the small animals that have eaten the algae, then even larger fish enter into this food chain. Finally people eat the larger fish, showing a dependence of each group upon the other. The pyramid-of-numbers diagram shows the importance of algae to animal life.

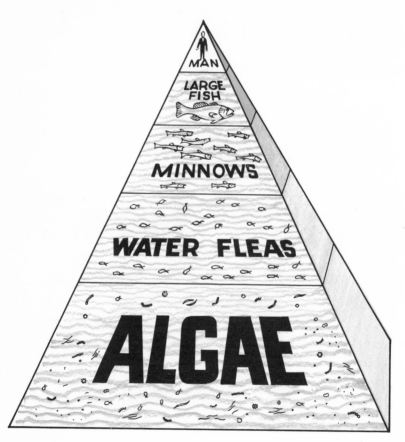

Algae provide food for people.

The Japanese and Chinese have eaten a great variety of marine green, red, and brown algae in salads, soups, and puddings for many years. In Japan a marine red alga is collected in nets placed in the ocean. The sheet-like, small plants are placed together on racks to dry and are sold as a common food called "nori." In New Brunswick, Canada, another marine red alga commonly called "dulse" is dried and packaged for sale in the grocery stores. It is used to flavor foods and can be cooked with milk and butter to make a stew with an oyster flavor. Another marine red alga is used to thicken soups in Ireland.

Eventually algae may become an even more important source of food for man.

One of the ingredients often used in salad dressing is taken from brown algae. This substance is called "alginate" (*al*-juh-nate). Similar to gelatin, alginates have the ability to soak up liquids and to gel. They may also be added to puddings, chocolate milk, and ice cream—giving these foods a smoother texture.

A jellylike substance called "carrageenen" (kare-uh-*gee*-nun), produced from two marine red algae, may be added to chocolate milk, eggnog, ice cream, flavored syrups, frostings, jellies, soups, and some baked goods. Carrageenen gives a smooth texture to these products.

Algae are a source of medicine.

A marine red alga has been used for many years in Greece to free people of internal worms. Another is used to treat sore throats. Products made from algae are used in dressing wounds and are useful in skin grafting and lung and brain surgery. Carrageenen is used in salves and ointments. Recent research has shown that certain algae produce antibiotics which will destroy many bacteria that can cause illness in both people and animals.

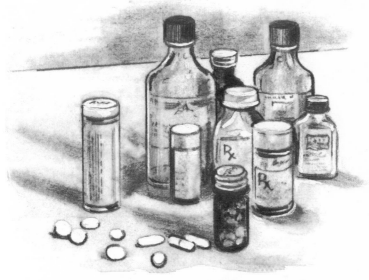

Red algae produce agar, a substance used in treating stomach disorders. However, the most important use of agar is in a gel-like medium made for the growth of bacteria and other microorganisms. The agar serves as food in which microscopic forms of life can grow.

Agar is also used to make the capsules that hold medicine and vitamins.

Algae help other plants grow.

Certain blue-green algae can take nitrogen gas from the air, converting it into chemicals to make the soil more fertile, and increase the growth of crops such as beans and potatoes. Phycologists (fy-*col*-o-gists), people who study about algae, have been able to double the rice crop in India and Japan by growing certain blue-green algae in the water-covered fields before planting the rice.

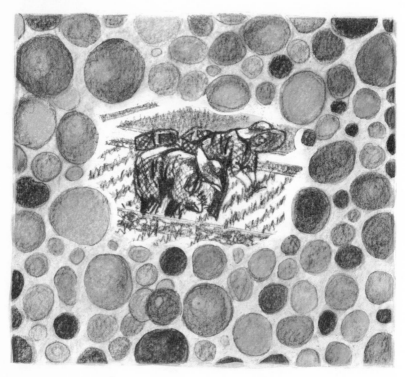

In New Zealand, Ireland, Great Britain, Canada, and Norway brown algae have been powdered or liquified and used as fertilizer for crops.

38

Algae are useful in scientific research.

Because the algae can be grown more easily and more rapidly than many other forms of life, they are very suitable for use in laboratories. Algae serve as laboratory "guinea pigs." They are used to study poisons, to determine nutritional or food requirements, and to learn more about living processes and causes of death.

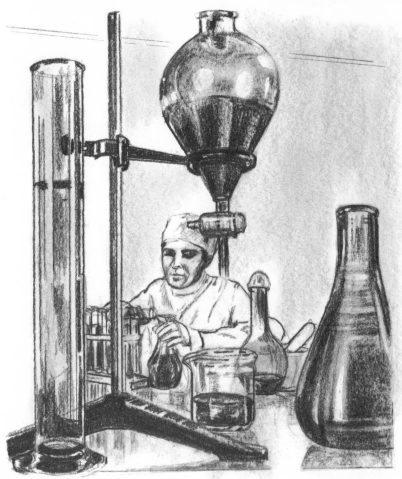

Algae are collectors of chemicals.

Algae are important in biofiltration (bi-o-fil-*tra*-shun), the using of microscopic plants to remove chemicals from polluted water.

Iodine, calcium, and phosphorus are chemicals which can be removed from water by algae, which concentrate them in or on their bodies.

I Ca P

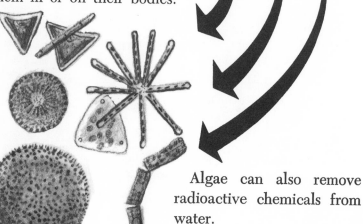

Algae can also remove radioactive chemicals from water.

40

Diatoms are a unique group of algae because they live in "glass houses." The cell walls of diatoms are like tiny glass shells called frustules (*frus*-chules). There are thousands of kinds of diatoms. Each kind has a frustule with a different shape or markings. The shells may be shaped like boats, needles, discs, or vertebrae.

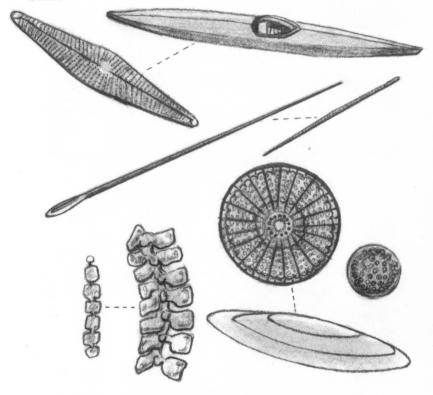

The markings are so delicate that they may be seen only with the very best microscopes.

Some diatoms float in the water, drifting with the currents. Others attach themselves to sticks, stones, and larger plants in the water.

The diatoms have many uses. They serve as food for many animals living in the lakes and oceans. Diatoms aid in purifying water by collecting silica and other chemicals from the water to build their frustules and by producing oxygen. They manufacture oils and protein. Scientists believe that the diatoms played an important role in the formation of petroleum deposits over a period of millions of years.

Diatomaceous (die-uh-toe-*may*-shus) earth is earth containing diatom shells of golden-brown algae that originally lived in water. The shells were gradually deposited on the ocean floor in massive layers—several hundred feet thick—as the diatoms died. In time, as changes were made upon the land, the oceans receded; and the diatomaceous earth became a part of the earth's surface.

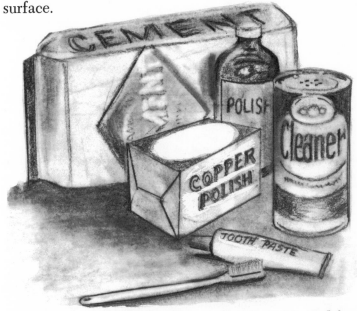

Much of this diatomaceous earth is found in California. The deposits extend many miles, and some are as much as a half mile deep.

Diatomaceous earth is used for polishes, filters, and insulating materials. Cement becomes stronger when diatomaceous earth is added to it.

You may have some of this earth formed from algae shells in your home. It is often used in packages of household cleansers and in some toothpaste.

43

PROBLEMS CAUSED BY ALGAE

Some of the algae can be harmful to people. Drinking water can have a fishy or earthy taste because of the presence of certain algae, along with bacteria and mold, in the water. Some of the blue-green algae, when growing in large quantities in water, can produce toxic, or poisonous, chemicals in sufficient amounts to cause sickness or death to animals drinking it.

Heavy growths of blue-green algae may indicate polluted water.

A large film of floating algae on a fishpond may cause the death of fish, since their oxygen supply will be used by the plants at night. The blanket of algae will also cut off the light supply from the atmosphere, and algae living below the blanket will not produce oxygen.

Certain algae, when growing in large enough quantity to color the water—a condition called "red tide"—produce enough poison to kill millions of fish and other animals. Shellfish such as clams and snails are not killed when eating the algae, but they become a source of illness, sometimes resulting in death, for people who eat the shellfish.

ALGAE MAY HELP US EXPLORE SPACE

Biologists are studying the ways that algae may be of importance in space explorations. They believe one type of algae may be grown in sufficient amounts to help maintain whole space colonies.

In space the algae could help provide an atmosphere and food. People would breathe the oxygen the plants give off. In turn, the plants could use the carbon dioxide that people exhale. Algae would combine the carbon dioxide with nitrogen gas to make their plant foods.

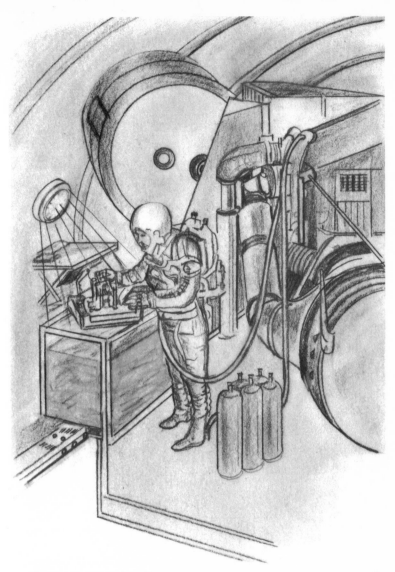

Algae have also been important in space research programs by providing much information about food manufacture, vitamin production, oxygen yields, and growth rates under different conditions.

SUMMARY

Algae are living organisms that are found almost everywhere. They are most often found in water and soil, although they also live on surfaces exposed to the air and in or on other plants and animals. They have a great variety of colors, shapes, and sizes. They may be studied just as they grow in nature, or they may be placed in growth media to be studied more closely with a hand lens or a microscope.

Most algae are classified as plants because they possess chlorophyll and make their own food. The five major divisions of algae are made on the basis of color. Algae may reproduce asexually or sexually.

Certain algae are used as food and medicine for animals and people. They are used as fertilizers to help other plants grow. They are useful in scientific research. Algae produce oxygen for animals and plants. They are important in the cleaning of polluted water. Some algae may also pollute the water.

Algae are most important in that they serve as the basic food in one of the food chains involving animals, from invisible forms to man.